The Natural Resources of My Community

Elliot Paderewsk

Rosen REAL READERS

Rosen Classroom™
New York

This is my family. We use **natural resources**. A natural resource is something that can be found in nature and used by people.

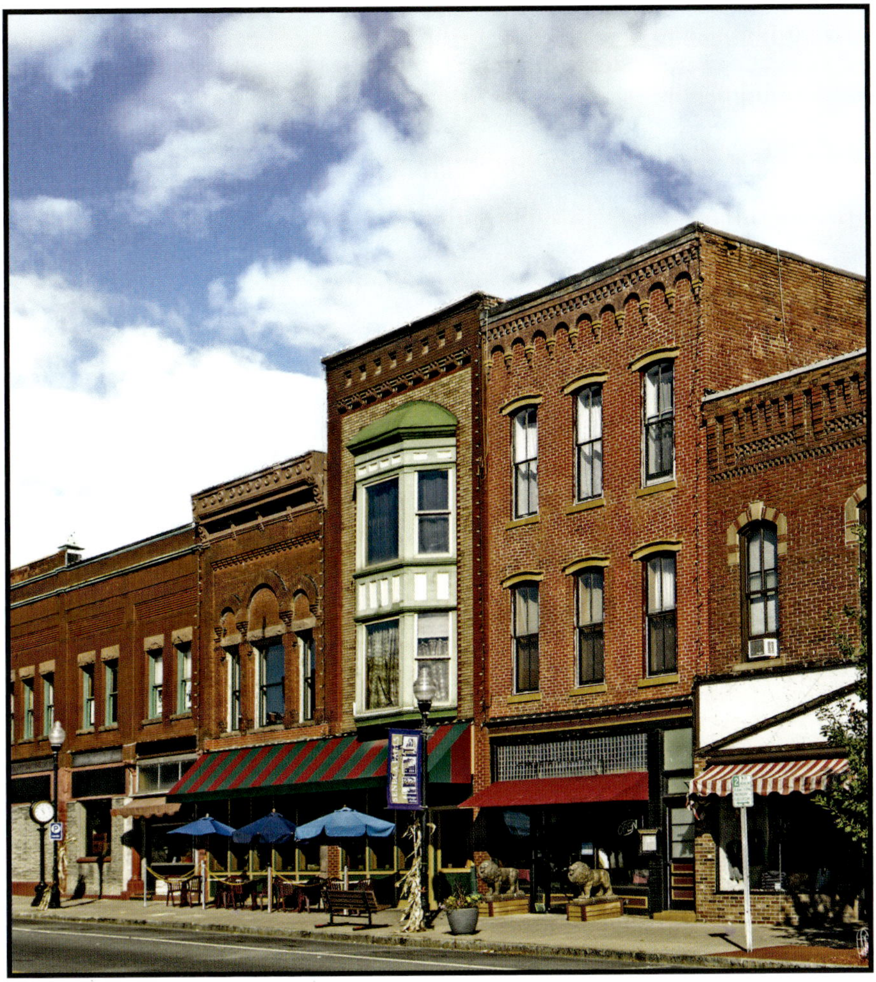

Natural resources are important. They are used in our day-to-day lives. There are many natural resources in our community.

Natural resources are all around us. They include the air that we breathe and the soil in the ground.

Plants that grow in the ground are natural resources. Plants give off **oxygen**. We need oxygen to live.

There are many trees in our community. Trees are an important natural resource. Wood from trees is used to make things.

Mom and Dad go to the local gas station to put **gas** in their cars. Cars run on gas. Gas is a natural resource.

Sunlight is also a natural resource. Some houses in our community have **solar panels** on top of them. Solar panels absorb sunrays and make energy.

Water is one of our most important natural resources. We need to drink water to live. We have access to water in our community.

We have farms in our community. Many natural resources are found on farms. Farm animals are natural resources.

We eat food that comes from farms. Natural resources play an important part in our lives. We need some natural resources to live. Others help to make our lives better.

Glossary

gas A liquid mixture used as fuel for a car.

natural resource Something that is found in nature and can be used by people.

oxygen A chemical in the air that people breathe and need to live.

solar panel A panel that absorbs sunrays and makes energy.